Living With a Reason

Tori Silver

BookLeaf Publishing

Presentation by *BookLeaf Publishing*

Web: www.bookleafpub.com

E-mail: info@bookleafpub.com

ISBN: 9789357617802

First edition 2022

This book is dedicated to my ever loving and supportive wife Kirsty, my two beautiful daughters Cosima and Asha and any future family additions we may be lucky enough to have.

I love you all.

You, are My Reason.

ACKNOWLEDGEMENT

Human beings. We are all human beings.
We are not distinguished by the anatomy which lies at the apex of our thighs.
We are not validated by the tempered disillusions of the narrow-minded.
We are not born into this world as mortal enemies and we should not
develop into a divided race.
We are all souls living on a planet called Earth, our home.
We are for all intents and purposes a community.
We should act as such.
Every individual has an equal right to exist and thrive.
Every individual has an equal right to love and be loved.
Every individual has an equal right to be valued.
It is about time we accept this and welcome our fellow souls.
Be kind, be appreciative, be you.
Love yourself, love others and value everyone.

I am so grateful for my life's journeys, no matter how many it feels like I've had. Thank you for reading, sharing, supporting in whatever way you have. It is all appreciated.

PREFACE

All of my life I have felt like I was battling the world, except the world was inside of me. At this moment I am thirty-one years old and it is only within the last year that I have really and truly started sharing the inner monologues of my life. The dreams, dramas, struggles, hurtful times and genuine abuse. There are things in the book that are hard to write, hard to read, hard to comprehend. And that's okay! Life is not about having everything together all of the time. There are reasons behind all of our journeys and every one is meant to be.

The impact we can have on ourselves and others is a motivating force. Use it wisely.

For an Attentive Audience

Reading articles, viewing documentaries highlighting the woes and pitfalls of society, I find myself feeling deeply for those in peril. I plead for change, claw for enlightenment and pray to any listening ears for an outburst of tenacious strength. Undoubtedly this is an era of downfall simply aching for an outcry of human decency on mass. Dictatorship caressing the outskirts of the world, piercing hatred and dishonour through the outer layers of safety. Turning my head I see it. My reflection looking back at me. Mascara cascading down my face in the wake of the overspill of my inner turmoil. Salty fluid burning its way down my lightly flushed skin, akin to the first ski trail in a fresh blanket of snow. Glancing back at the dishevelled image, tendrils of hair clinging to my face; I grimace at the sight. Not much different to any other day wherein I hide behind the false pretences of makeup as though living behind a comforting mask. I wipe my face and collect my thoughts.

If the world could see itself in the mirror. Truly take in its reflection. Able to analyse the trails of destruction, the languish of life, the harmful disregard to Mother Nature. Would it feel the same way we as people do when we see our own flaws? Would it crumble and allow the damage to become its ultimate demise? No, the Earth is a fighter. A creator. An optimistic ruler in the face of solemnity. The Earth would understand that its predisposed disposition for life, love and evolution is far greater than any means brought to light to cause disruptions to its path. It is, after all, home to a multitude of living organisms.

In the same way as the Earth, we as people should hold true to our predispositions. Our instilled awareness of self. Our innate ability to love and be loved.

I decide then and there that each one of us should look past the views of society. Ignore the inner negativity. Relish in the feeling of selfless activism. Don't be shut down by the tousled hair or indignant musings of the scars of our past. You are your own sacred creation. A beautiful soliloquy, passionately spoken for an attentive audience. You, as the Earth, are the centre of your very own universe. Live in the knowledge of your intriguing uniqueness. Love and be honest for yourself. Love and be brave for humanity.

You are decidedly important.

Live.

Anxiety or Infatuation // Delirious Living

Anxious or Infatuated?

Have you ever wondered how anxiety
can link in with the notion of love?
How calling your senses to sobriety
is sometimes barely enough?
The sweating palms and racing heart
Breathing erratic, out of sync
Never quite knowing where it starts
In too deep before you can think
No mustering up of your will power
Too far gone to call it a day
Lasts a second, one minute, an hour
Mind and body completely astray
It seems the physical attributions
Be they subconscious or pulled from your brain
All lead to the same infiltrations
Of drunken fluidity needing restrain
Now standing before these new faces
Leaves me shaking and forming a stutter
Yet only taking my departing paces
Do I realize I have yet to falter
It is then that I see the connection
Between anxiety and infatuation

For something that takes all your senses
Can begin a whole new revelation

—-----------

Why did I let you under my skin
You pushed me around yet I still let you in
Your gravity pulled but it brought me to hell
I promise myself no never again
The cries in the night and the thump in my chest
Running on low got no will power left
The tethers I'm seeing more frayed than before
No freedom no mercy no miracle cure
Help me or leave me don't tease me with words
Or drunken forgetting of putting me first
My feet on the ground aren't that stable for running
They're sore and they're weak and my bones just keep crumbling
So save me because I just can't save myself
It's like one day just maybe I'll go get some help
But there's tragedy and then there is reckless destruction
It's swept under rugs in abandon-less judgement
I'm worn down and damaged and torn from all sides
I'm deranged and I'm chided I'm blackened inside
I can see myself still in the dust and the ashes

But I'm falling and buried under rocks in their masses
If lightning could strike it would hit three times strong
It would use and abuse me yet string me along
I'd see each day anew with a glassier vision
All for the outcome of delirious living

A Friend to Me

You chose to see me,
For who I am inside.
You choose to see the person,
I no longer need to hide.
You choose to be upfront,
And say things to my face.
But you don't make me feel small,
And you're never on my case.

A lot of people come and go,
Throughout the life we lead.
Many are acquaintances,
Others, friends we need.

But what happens when that friendship,
Is pushed up to the gate?
A test of strength and honesty,
A sign of love or hate.

To know who your real friends are,
Is the greatest gift of all.
The ones who'll stay and help you up,
Recover your greatest fall.

You have your mates, your friends, your best,

Maybe some enemies.
But i have to say I'm truly blessed,
Because you're a friend to me.

October 2010

I am Woman // Poetry

I am a woman
I am strong and I'm powerful
Yet I'm weak with emotion
I feel and I fall and I stand far too strong
So that each person new to me
Sees me so wrong
I am a woman
I am fearless
But fear itself resides in everything I do
I jump with faith and wonder and determination
Yet I am still scared of my own truth
I am a woman
I am a safe-hold
I am the cabin of retreat when people need a haven of hope yet I find less and less in the eyes that look back at me
I am a woman
I am everything I need to be and everything I need not
From the top of my head to the soles of my feet I am fierce with abandon and reckless with force
I am a woman
And I love me

*Note that “I am woman” no longer stands as a statement for Tori

——------------

Poetry I hate you
You control me
Poetry I need you
You console me
Poetry I love you
You believe in me
Poetry fuck you
You destroy me

Poetry I want you
But you hurt me
Poetry I despise you
But you heal me
Poetry I crave you
But you withdraw from me
Poetry screw you
You ignore me

Poetry I feel you
You break me
Poetry I long for you
You calm me
Poetry I claim you
But you disown me

Poetry I believed in you
You swore to me

Poetry I write for you
You lie to me
Poetry I live for you
You mither me
Poetry I'd die for you
You revive me
Poetry I'm here for you
You define me

Only Human // Letter to Myself

They're back again
The nights of no sleep
Nothing helps, nothing hinders
No sound or no peep.

Help me turn it off
This brain it needs to quit
It won't let up it won't back down
I don't understand its "wit"

I survive on no sleep
I can go on for days
I'm sped up I'm slowed down
But always in a haze.

I get angry and frustrated
I can twitter on for hours
I can feel like I am worthless
Or like I have superpowers

Sometimes I'm creative
Other times I'm in the gutter
I can hold a conversation
Or simply have no words to utter

I can move like I'm a robot
But then float and feel the fall
All of it's exhausting
I'm only human after all.

—-----------

If I could write a letter to myself
It would say don't walk through hell with no help

If I could write a letter to my conscience
It would say don't listen to the people's nonsense

If I could write a letter to my inner voices
It would be about my inner soul and having choices

If I could have wrote a letter to my younger version
It would be to make yourself grow up the bigger person

If I wrote a letter to my own responsibilities
I would say don't be afraid to get dirt on your knees

If I wrote a letter every time I stumbled
Maybe it would teach me to be kinder to be humble

If I could or wrote a letter to the other sides of me
It would be a paragraph to stop myself from lying to me

If I wrote a letter to the doubt inside my brain
Maybe I would read it, maybe all my inner thoughts would change

If I wrote a letter with the same consistency
That you have inside you every time you're pissed at me

If I wrote a letter based on better choices
Maybe I could fight back and defeat the petty voices

If I wrote a letter dedicated to my royalties
You can bet your fucking ass that they'd be loyal to me

If I could of wrote a letter trying to make you understand
I wouldn't need to be before you with my heart inside my hand

If a letter's what it takes to make you care for me
Then I know you're not the one who does deserve me.

Done.

A letter of Goodbye

Inspired by a true life story heard on the radio on a rainy wednesday afternoon.

Damn it Dad, I miss you, the way we used to be.
Think about the good times, all the laughs, just you and me.
Do you even understand how my life has flipped around?
You don't even see me now, like a ghost, without a sound.
Tell me this, am I still, always your little girl?
Or has something over taken, the love inside your world?
Did you know me when I planned, to fall off of that bridge?
Or see the slashes on my wrists, no longer your kid.
Do you feel the way I do?
Can you see me now?
Hanging from this tree.
I have one question…How?

You let yourself get drunk, every single night.

And when you're kinda sober, you still start up a fight.
Dad please don't hit Mom, hit me instead, I'll take it.
Here, take my neck, just go ahead and break it.

I've seen the things you do, I've seen the way you act.
But now Dad you don't scare me, because now it's just a fact.
On Christmas you would wake us, give us a Daddy hug.
Now, fat chance, you make us lie face down on the rug.
The dog had all the sense, to up and run away.
But for us it's not that easy, you forced us all to stay.
Dad your fists are heavy, they beat me to the ground.
But as long as you don't hit Mom, it means I'll stick around.
…
Hey Dad.. Now it's over, you broke our hearts in two.
Now you can remember, all the laughs, just me and you.
You'll sit there all alone, and wallow in your drink.

And you'll cry at all the pictures; at least it'll make you think.
You messed your life up, mine and Moms, you ended both of ours.
So now you need to live with that, but you don't have the scars.
The emotions that you lack will all come to the surface now.
So I just have one question Dad…
Here's that one question…
How?

The Most Important Relationship

The most important relationship you will ever be in is the one with yourself.

Your understanding of yourself will constantly change as you grow and build upon your foundations of knowledge, just as your ability to draw connections to the world around you will become more apparent. You live life with expectations based upon the groundings of society and the history that comes along with it. Our fore-people have built a conscious pathway for us to travel on, but we will inherently keep digging, keep building and keep making new discoveries. Each and every one of us has a past. Each and every one of us has an ancestral connection with some form of freedom fighter. No matter the culture you are born into, the country you reside or the race in which your skin depicts; you have a story.

As humans, we identify with those whom we feel a connection with. Connections reside regardless of our background or our upbringing.

There are people you will meet in life that will become more important to the growth of your soul than someone you perceived to be what you needed. There are people you will never meet, yet you will be influenced by them in a way you would have thought to be unattainable. Influential beings are all around us and they nourish our souls and our growth in ways we may not even recognise. These are the people we value in our journey to love and discovery. These are the people we are in an unlabeled relationship with. This is true love.

Love in the conventional sense is seen to be something shared between partners, or family members, or platonic friends. Love is seen to be both a healer and a destroyer of connections. Love is seen to be the most powerful force we as humans are capable of permitting. There is just one problem with all of these notions: they do not see the value of loving yourself. Our society as it stands pushes the belief that the connection with others is more beneficial to our health and growth than anything, yet it does not take into consideration how important it is to love yourself. Self-value should be at the forefront of any person's life skills menagerie.
Self-knowledge should be at the forefront of

growth. Self-awareness at the forefront of intuition and self-love is the base of life.
It should not be seen that your value is more important than any other person on this planet, yet you should undoubtedly value yourself enough to prove to other people that you are undeniably important. To truly show and receive love, you first need to appreciate your own worth and love yourself for all that you are and all that you have been. Knowing yourself for everything you have is life's biggest achievement, but loving yourself for all that comes with it can be life's biggest struggle.

To love yourself, all sides of you, in each and every corner and under each and every social umbrella is truly the most rewarding relationship you will ever find yourself in. It is the relationship that will help you grow, encourage you to challenge the world around you and increase your ability to love and appreciate others. It is this relationship that will bring you to a realization that you yourself can be that influential human to those who meet you and those who never will.

Making your relationship with yourself the most important one for you, will be the best decision you have ever made.

Learn about you.
Accept you.
Value you.
Praise you.
Be you.
Love you.

Touched with Fire // Gravity Pulling

Flatten all the hurt
And squash all the rumours
They make you despise
The fortune of others

A full healthy heart
Is the key to success
Without any love
Every life is a mess

A world as a team
Is strong beyond belief
When there's a hardship
We can all bring relief

A confidence boost
For yourself to inspire
All other people
Who have been 'Touched with Fire'

05.05.2011

—----------

Dangerous lives and dangerous minds
To venture and wander
To scurry and hide

To box it all off
In one big apartment
To hide perfect sins
In secret compartments

Tragedy, sorrows, forgiveness and dread
Elation, great wellness, light soul and clear head

A path of no mercy
We follow and fly
To live is to live
Not to pause 'til we die

A gravity pulling
In every direction
A master at none
Only skill is deflection

Suspicion, a curse, humanity's flaws
Take a hold, grab your steed, own what is yours
Be that hunger or thirst
Be that glee or recoiling
Like the ice that is frozen
Or hell where it's boiling

The sorrow you feel is the true desperation
For happiness, sadness, depression, elation.

"BUT YOU LOOK FINE"

When it's four am and the insomnia has gotten you to the point where you can't function, you struggle the next day to even verbalise simple words. "But you look fine"

When you're screaming in pain and there's no given cure or way to relieve it yet you wait until it passes before seeing other people. "But you look fine"

When the doctors tell you there's a possibility you'll never have children so you go through internal hell every day being surrounded by reminders of a life you're scared you'll never have. "But you look fine"

When you experience physical paralysis because your brain decides to take a break every now and again yet you still find a way to be independent. "But you look fine"

When you drop into seizures unannounced from the simplest of things like being too hot or tired and you lose all your senses. "But you look fine"

When your voice box forgets how to work and you lose all ability to speak and are left with just producing noises to try and express yourself it destroys you. “But you look fine”

When you push your nearest and dearest away because you just don’t feel worthy. “But you look fine”

When your limbs don’t work and your heart beats so hard in your chest it feels like it’s jumping out of your rib cage. “But you look fine”

When you hear every day that your job is on the line if you don’t start sorting your health even though you’re dealing as best you can. “But you look fine”

When you’re weak on your feet and the only option is to use crutches just to get around the house but are too embarrassed to be seen as weak outside. “But you look fine”

When you know you need to take a break and stop pushing yourself but you refuse to rely on other people so push yourself to work anyway and no one actually gets it. “But you look fine”

When you're wiping the tears with every step you take and every cup you carry through the pain. "Because you look fine"

Aces aren't Aces // Love is Louder

Living on nothing is all but a dream
To follow the holy, to hide but be seen
The rich and the wealthy there's nothing of such
To draw from the heart and the soul is enough
Levels and layers and depths from afar
But close up they see it's just not who you are
A traveller backpacking, living the journey
When inside it is screaming;can nobody hear me?
Persona is one thing and person another
The game faces hides person that needs to recover
Perform it and drain you just go do your act
Too spaced out to function or grasp any fact
No sleeping, no eating, total disregard
A perfect bravado, your number one card
The ace in your pack, the last one to play
But aces aren't aces when given away
Re-live it don't waste it now hold on to life
Through hunger and pain and through constant strife
Do not let them see you, keep up the pretend
There's always improvements, you'll die at the end

—------------

Danger is round every corner
Danger it lurks out of sight
It strikes when people aren't looking
It comes with all of its might

In shadows and thoughts it lingers
Whirling inside your own head
Watching and waiting it ponders
Secretly wishing you dead

It forms as an accident one day
The next a slip or a fall
But slowly it builds in the back of your mind
Until you can't take it at all

You muster the courage and try
To break out your very own skin
You take to the sharpest of pieces
Hoping that you might just win

You wish that the battle was over
The battle between you and yourself
The fight pouring out with a crimson touch
But you stop and put it on the shelf

You realise things need to change

And what is broken needs to be fixed
The love that is precious around you
Are feelings not to be mixed

To the back of your mind all the hatred
And the thoughts that brought all the harm
Because love is louder than anything
Love can keep the world calm.

It Wasn't Your Fault // Not Mine

When you see the lashes on my wrists,
Or the scar around my neck,
You will soon know, that long ago,
I took a brush with death.

It wasn't your fault,
It was all in my head,
To see you with her,
I'd rather be dead.

I had it all,
You took it away,
And life was so hard
I wouldn't live another day.

She was my all,
My soul and my friend,
We said we'd be together,
Until the very end.

She fell for you hard,
She just couldn't see,
That what she was doing,
Was ruining me.

—----------

Confide in me,
And let me heal you

Believe in my heart,
And i can cure your sadness

Trust in my loyalty,
And I can heal your pain

Have faith in my love,
And leave all doubts behind

A strong heart, an open mind,
And gently let your fears subside.

You by my side,
The warmth of your touch.

You are all I want,
And all I need.

You are my thoughts,
And all of my dreams.

You are my life,
And what keeps me alive.

You are all I have,
And yet you are not mine.

The Diary of an Empath

The diary of an empath surely seems
Like a lot of emotion and too many dreams
But a diary is more than the writing of feelings
It is but a gateway to musings and meanings

A soliloquy that, you can find, if you please,
Is carefully balanced but not with such ease
As it all but contains an ocean of sorts
A serene yet tumultuous blending of thoughts.

It is moulded together by pen and a pad
It describes and encompasses both happy and
sad
But the treacherous details are not but one story
Yet rather a gathering of haphazard glory

For being an empath, as blesses it may be
Is a torturous journey like saling the sea
As your body and brain soak the energies on
mass
Your resolve and self-loving become frail as
glass.

The bitter, the love, the hurt and the worry

Ebb deep in your veins, flowing through in a
hurry
On daily a basis you feel physically drained
Because switching through temperaments leaves
you pained

You find your way to creatively let
Because every night you're not nearly done yet
So, you push on and hope with all you hold
dearly
You're reading the diary of an empath, clearly.

What it Meant to Cry // What am I thankful for?

No one ever told me what it meant to cry.

Tell me how to feel
Tell me how to cry
Tell me how to live my life
Or tell me how to die

After all the telling
A moment just might do
To look upon the open life
And find just me and you

I feel like I'm a cancer
For me there is no cure
Infecting those around me
Those who used to be so pure

Let's have one more minute
To see what this has cost
Memories of a household
For a love that can't be lost

A friend is all I ask for
One friend, that's not too much

A single soul in all the world
To provide that special touch

The feeling one can only get
When a spark is passed between
An energy you can’t forget
Can’t forge, or fake, but mean.

Where is this one friend?
When did my life fall flat?
Does friendship have to end?
Is it really all that?

Am I hung up on something
That is really not that much
Maybe there’s no energy
Nor that special touch

But I remember feeling it
I’d know it all the same
If it ever crossed my path once more
If I was lucky enough again

Let me find that friendship
Let me wait and see
The cure is what I’m seeking
From this cancer that is me.

All I ask is one thing

One thing, not too much
Let friendship be the answer
Let me find that special touch.

—----------

I am thankful for the moments
That are never real goodbyes
And all those precious times
When you laugh instead of cry

I am thankful for the meaning
Behind a special kiss
And the moment when a feeling
Is that of pure bliss

I'm thankful for the people
Who light our very souls
And the young ones who appreciate
The wisdom of the old

I am thankful for good friendship
For food and drink and time
I am thankful for the memories
That play inside my mind

I am thankful for the people
Who put their life in front of harm
To protect us and to save us

And to keep us pure at heart

I am thankful for the children
Who are miracles at birth
And to all of the young midwives
Who strive to prove their worth

I am thankful when it seems
Like all have lost their faith
For the ones who stand up tall
And do what's needed on the day

I am thankful, to be honest
For those who understand
How a difference in a quality
Means no difference in a man

I am thankful for the judgeless
For the rich that help the poor
I am thankful for the hopeful
For always being sure

I am thankful for survivors
When someone broke their trust
And for the ones that pulled it back
When the world seemed just too much

I am thankful to be writing
To have my health and heart

I am thankful if this letter
Makes you think or helps your heart

I am thankful for the heroes
That this world has gave birth to
For amongst all of the thankfulness
A hero lies in you.

The Realisation // Is This Love?

As you slept I could not
I stood trembling, lost in thought

You on one side, me on the other
Yet I blushed when I pulled back the covers

I slid in carefully under the sheets
Praying our skin would not touch or meet

My heart racing out of control
Wanting to have you, wanting to hold

Feeling every vein in my body pulse with that relentless beat
Like a volcano wanting to erupt, surging with heat

Pulling the pillows and the sheets up tight
Feeling the urge to flee or fight

Nowhere to run, nowhere to hide
Trying to fight this need inside

I've overcome this battle of pain and lust

And won something more important, her trust

—-------------

I feel drunk but I've not touched one drop
Heart is pounding there's no way to turn
Desperate searching can't find my way up
Am I drowning in air? Am I choking?

Is this love, 'cause it feels like an ocean
Tides and waves just pulling me down
And I can't seem to push from the bottom back up
Is this love?
I don't want it right now.

Tell me, are these emotions too real?
Are they raw as they cut through your soul?
Do they bring in a flood of new melodies?
Does it feel like you're hot but you're cold?

Touch me like you do when we're dancing
Look at me like I might break
Admire me just like an artwork
One that's yours, that's no one's to take

Is this love, 'cause it feels like a river
Ebbs and flows but only waist deep
I can't seem to wade to the bankside

Is this love? I don’t think I want it.

Look me dead in the eyes and feel nothing
Don’t linger or look at my lips
You can’t do it, i feel you wanting
My breath on your neck and smile as we kiss

I’d say tell me that you don’t need me
But I know you’d giggle because you can’t lie
Electricity flows right between us
It’s visible to all on the outside

Is this love ‘cause it feels neverending
Heart is pounding inside of my chest
And I stay breathing softly to ease it
Is this love?
I feel it somehow.

In the simplest touch I get breathless
In your eyes I can see all the stars
In your smile I could fight off an army
But your mind holds the key to my heart.

Is this love?
It feels like an ocean.
Tides and waves are just part of the swell.
I don’t want to push.
At the bottom I’m stuck.
Is this love?

I sure hope so.
Is this love?
Well…

The 'Joys' of Life // The Art of Loss

I may be still a little young
But boy how time does fly
The future is a foreign thing
But with you by my side
I'll find the strength to conquer
All of life's adversities
And your love will help solve all of
The weak inside of me.

So like I said I'm still twenty
But man I've had my share
Of struggles and a lot of pain
In life, my own warfare.
But time goes on apparently
For me this does not seem
To be the case or even so
It feels I cannot dream.

I tend to just revert back to
My old ways of coping
Instant release upon myself
The feeling that it brings.
Even though I may cherish life
Habits don't up and go

I don't regret my past at all
And one day you'll all know.

Until that day I'll keep hiding
The cuts, a scar, a bruise.
And never tell a soul who talks
Or asks what 'tools' I use.
I'll keep upon my face a mask
Of smiles, hide how I feel.
And confidence will act as my
Escape from what is real.

05.05.2011

—--------

Losing someone's physicality hurts. It breaks you down and leaves a gaping loss in the centre of your heart. Your head filled solely with the memories of them, trying to grasp the dull concept that you will never again be in their presence. No more lingering gazes. No more comfort from their touch. No more deep breaths against their neck, or inhaling their scent. No longer able to feel their heart beating in time with yours.
It is a definite.
An end.

When you lose someone's essence, you flail. A cumbersome trail of thoughts clouding your everyday outlook. Nowhere to turn for the answers, you guide yourself towards your neverending nothingness. It is when you lose a person's essence that you truly lose them. As they are, 'your person'. You lose them, and in doing so, lose yourself.
It is hard to fathom the reason as to why we so heavily rely on other individuals in life. But really the answer is simple. To shape you. To mould you. To teach you and keep you safe.
Without experience we are nothing.
Without the art of loss, we would never find gratitude or compassion.
Without gratitude and compassion, we are barely human.

I hope you can see the Moon // Today I caught the Sun

I hope you can see the moon
How beautiful she can be
I hope you look upon her
The way she looks down on me
I hope you're up there with the stars
And that's why they shine so bright
I hope the flicker in their glow
Is you dancing in the night
I hope you speak to the moon like me
And tell her secrets I told you
I hope that when she hears my voice
You're listening with her too
I hope you know I feel you here
Even though you're not around
I hope you know I hear your voice
Even though there is no sound
I hope one day I'll see you again
But one day far from this
Because even though I still feel pain
It's a pain I'd sort of miss
Because pain in this way shapes me
It makes me value my time
This pain that comes from loving
Is a pain that I'm glad is mine

So I thank you for teaching me laughter
And unconditional love
For teaching me pride and honour
I thank you, for all the above

——--------------

Today I caught the Sun
The Moon she wasn't happy
The stars, they said "let's go to bed, there's no use feeling crappy"
"But look at her," the Moon cried. "She's brown and toasty warm"
"I can't do that and that's a fact, so now I feel forlorn"
The Moon she sighed and left
Into the light of day
The Sun she saw and then she felt
A pang of sheer dismay
The Sun made a decision
For now and evermore
Each day she'd die
At night she'd hide
Of that she was for sure.
The Moon she loved the Sun
Each day she'd take her leave
The Sun she loved the Moon so much
She dies to let her breathe.

She Is...

She sees the moon
As it passes in the night sky
She speaks to it though she knows there will never be an answer
She sees the beauty there that sometimes gets forgotten and vows to tell her every day
Because she is magic
She knows that without the moon there are no water tides and without tides there is no life
So she tells her
She says "You're beautiful. You do not need the sun to compare to be you, as yourself can stand alone and bask in your glory and wonder"
The moon replies the only way she knows how
She lights her way through the dark and guides her home
Holds her in her arms as though she were her lover and keeps her safe from storms
The moon takes the love with all the gratitude she can muster even though she herself does not value her beauty
She knows her part to play and does it well, she reminds herself
"I am far away and up close you would not think or say the things you do because you would see

my grey palette and the craters left by worldly
collisions"
But she can see, she can see clearly and truly
and she can feel and love and hold her close
each night
She can see it in the way the moon smiles back
in that way that only she knows
She can feel it in the way the moon glows when
it's dark
She can hold her dearly and radiate in the
knowledge that the moon is not distant or cold or
even coloured in a grey dusty palette, but is all
the colours blended into a shining silver
For the moon is hers to have and hers to keep
And the moon who once did not, would not,
could not believe this to be true just feels it. She
shines brighter when her vision is blessed by her.
She moves more tides when her smile beams
brightly. She asks the stars to join her in
serenading all that is true and pure and she just
gets it.
For she is life and she is wonder and she is
home.

Overcoming

In life there are times when you will find
That some people are evil within
For they push you and pull you and lay their hands on you
And they do it all with a sick grin

I've felt the deception, the anger the hurt
I've felt the blood drip down my thighs
When for one solid minute they plunge the knife in
Then destroy your trust with their lies

There's a stigma attached to the words 'rape' and 'raped'
Makes it hard to move on from it happening
See for me they are memories, so painful, so raw
Ruins each piece of you, leaving you stinging

I won't say the ages, the names, or their genders
I won't even say where they live
But I will say that one thing's for certain so hear me
You took what was mine only to give

With hushed words said between you “No she likes it, go on”
And my cries drowning under your hand
My heart it was breaking, my honour was taken
When you’d finished I struggled to stand

Now it wasn’t the first time, not even the last
And it wasn’t like you were alone
But you did this to me, took my phone, trapped me in
Convinced everyone else I was home

But I wasn’t ‘home’ was I? I never was there
I just cleaned and obeyed and I cried
When your violent behaviour caused bloodshed, you traitor!
I managed to smile, leave and lie

To my family, my friends but again and again
I did it I never was free
From your vile evil torture, you watched me, I saw you
You’d follow me, stalk me, I couldn’t flee

This is the first time I’ve written about
What you did, I hate you all!
For you broke me, destroyed me, your faces they haunt me
Now my Wife picks me up when I fall.

I still panic in darkness, I recoil from some touches
And rarely I look at myself, with compassion, forgiveness,
for what happened, you did this
You ruined intimacy for my soul.

What is the World? // Love Wins

Stand up for human rights. Fight for what you believe in. Unless all you believe in is your own wanton needs for societal standing, in which case I advise you to take one or two determined steps back and reevaluate the appreciation you have for the privileged life you lead.
We do not have an infinite lifeline to this planet. We do not own the rights to be an all consuming conglomerate, controlling the people as though in a production line.
We do however have EVERY RIGHT to take to platforms and let our voices be heard. We should fight for our rights and fight for people who have had their rights taken away. We should know that no matter what you are, who you are or where you are from, we are all living under the same universal treaty.
We find a home in this universe, a gaseous ball of energy softly floating within a galaxy. This home gives us a place to dream, to hope, to love. What is the world without the proper gratitude and appreciation for the beauty around us? What is the world we love in if not a safe haven from

the harsh fictitious imaginings created through social power?
We ALL deserve a right to live in harmony.
Do not let misconceptions fool you. There is no reason for negativity towards other humans.
There is no truth behind segregation.
We are one and together we will stand.

——-----------

Does it bother you that we live in a society of dreams, but the pompous acts of power leave it fraying at the seams?
Does it hinder your abilities to run, laugh, scream or sing, with destructive acts or terror so heavily debilitating?
Does it make you choke on words that once used to flow so freely, when the media and people dictate how you should be feeling?
Does it dampen your horizon or claw down at your faith, because the overwhelming narcissists are putting into place
Some quite dramatic and albeit narrow-minded laws and bans, leaving humans fleeing scared to even look or touch two hands.
Does it don the look of horror into tiny hope-filled eyes, when the children see the world through empty promises and lies?

If any of these mentioned have struck a chord or nerve, then don't sit back and watch, let's throw the world a curve
Ball, and ban the negativities and hinder righteous paths, let all people hold their hands and let the children have their laughs.
I do not want to be silenced, so I'm speaking these words freely.
Now nonsensical opinions just don't matter to me really. We are one in this together, humans true and humans strong. Stamping out destructive undertones and moving right along. Dousing flames with positivity and ridding worldly sins. Because a world I want to live in is a world in which Love Wins!

Happiness Found // Struck Gold

Her breath on my back
Her arms wrapped around me
Reminding me that the safest place on Earth
Is with her

The touch of her lips
Both power and passion
They teach me that promises can be made
In her kiss

The smile on her face
Unconditional gratitude
Understanding the comfort of knowing
She is mine

Hearing her voice
My new favourite sound
She is wonder, she is light, she is everything
My happiness has been found

July 5th 2018 22:33pm

——------------

How I know you love me
It's there each and every day
You rarely tell me with your words
But actions give you away

The soft hand on my back
Reassuring as I go
The way I catch you watching me
You think that I don't know

When you wake up in the morning
And a smile is the first thing
Or I mention what I'm craving
So you'll get it, buy or bring

You keep factoring me in things
I don't even think you realise
But it's there when breath gets lost
Or we can't look away from the other's eyes

I didn't really believe it
That you could ever like me
I was oblivious of course
But everyone else seemed to see

Apparently, it's electric
This 'spark' we seem to hold
I guess i could say I'm lucky
Yes it's cheesy, but I've struck gold.

My Word to My Wife // So Lay With Me

Darling you have been there
For me through all of this
You haven't asked for anything
Expected not one kiss

You truly do amaze me
You're so genuinely kind
I feel as though you treat me
Like you've known me for all time

Seeing as though you'ev helped
And listened to my cries
I thought that you should know
I will never tell you lies

You're special to me now
I never thought it would be so
But I never want to lose you
I want all this to show

So I'll make sure I remember
To keep my promises
And be there for you forever

You have my word on this

—-----------

In a strange way it hurts every time I look at you
because I know I will never be enough
It's like taking that shot of tequila knowing it
will burn on the way down but relishing in the
effects of the alcohol
It's like climbing a mountain knowing you'll
pass out but wanting just a glimpse of the
breathtaking view from the top
Laying with you burns as though I'm submerged
in a scolding bath just to ease the tension in my
muscles
Hearing your laugh flips my stomach until I am
sick from the joy it brings
But seeing your smile and knowing I caused it
tears my heart from its place in my chest and
throws it on the ground for you to step on

But it's worth it
Because it is yours
And the pain isn't really pain but it is all the
forms of beautiful torture arranged into what we
call •love•

So lay with me
Intertwine our fingers until we fall asleep

Laugh until our sides hurt and tears flow down our faces
Stay in my line of vision for as many minutes possible each day
And smile.
Smile that beautiful smile and tear my heart out because with you I know it's safe

March 14th 2018

www.ingramcontent.com/pod-product-compliance
Lightning Source LLC
Chambersburg PA
CBHW062147160726
48282CB00027B/951
9789357617802